Better Than Nice
and Other
Unconventional Prayers

Better Than Nice and Other Unconventional Prayers

Frederick Ohler

WJKP
Westminster/John Knox Press
Louisville, Kentucky

Book design by Gene Harris

First edition

Published by Westminster/John Knox Press
Louisville, Kentucky

PRINTED IN THE UNITED STATES OF AMERICA

9 8 7 6 5 4 3 2 1

Library of Congress Cataloging-in-Publication Data

Ohler, Frederick, 1931–
    Better than nice and other unconventional prayers / Frederick Ohler. — 1st ed.
        p.   cm.
    ISBN 0-664-21880-6

    1. Prayers.   I. Title.
BV245.036   1989
242′.8—dc20
                                                            89-8976
                                                              CIP

To Beverly—

my fiercest advocate,

truest love,

best friend

Contents

Illustrations

Illustration concept and selection by Lisa Ohler (LO); lithography camera work by Pete Tolleson, Warren Wilson College (WWC) Press.

A Chorus Beyond Hallelujah	Lithograph direct from a butterfly
As Good as Your Word	Definition of "be" from *The American Heritage Dictionary* (Boston: Houghton Mifflin Company, 1976), p. 114.
Better Than Nice	"ah lleluia," typeset in Avant Garde on a Macintosh computer
Blessed Untime	Nineteenth-century mortised cut
Except We Become	Photo of Chrisann Ohler, WWC, by Beverly Ohler
Extraordinary Moments/ Ordinary Lives	Photo of Gordon Mahy and Amy Stock, WWC, by Greg Harris
Extravagant God	"Various plants, including members of the Sumac, Spurge and Gourd families," botanical engraving by J. G. Heck, originally published in 1851.
From Breakfast to the Eschaton	Photo of fruit in the Saturday morning marketplace, Lausanne, Switzerland (LO)
I Want a Miracle	Lithograph direct from Queen Anne's lace *(Daucus carota)*
Life Is God-sized	Photo of tree, Lausanne (LO)
None So Blind	Photo of two plaster busts on an art class shelf, Lausanne (LO)
Providence	Photo of a passageway, Lausanne (LO)
Second Sight	Lithograph direct from a withered leaf

The Fullness Thereof	Photo of Barney the cat, WWC, by Chrisann Ohler
The Sun Thanks You Burning	"etc . . ." typeset in Caslon Antique
Ubiquity	Photo of a tree in winter, Lausanne (LO)
When the Deprivation's Done	Photo of the door of 14 Avenue Fraisse, from the inside looking out, Lausanne (LO)
Wholly Beautiful	Photo of Virginia Rath, WWC, by Greg Harris

Foreword

This manuscript has finally materialized after years of comments like "You really should publish some of Fred's words" and "You mean his work isn't in print *anywhere?*" Three decades of very special church services have touched, inspired, and unsettled people from all over the world who somehow managed to discover the Warren Wilson Presbyterian Church, tucked in the mountains of western North Carolina.

The church is located on the campus of Warren Wilson College, a small liberal arts school known for its student work program. Its congregation is a unique blend of students from Kenya to California, physics professors and dairy farmers, and people retired from jobs on the other side of the earth. Although both church and school are affiliated with the Presbyterian Church (U.S.A.), people of all faiths (Christian and non-Christian)—as well as those who don't consider themselves as professing any particular faith—are attracted to the unique, honest preaching of Fred Ohler. The words of his sermons and prayers are simple and their truths profound. He is often self-effacing, always searching; he asks questions more often than he gives answers, and in the process he has helped many in their own searches. People often comment that Fred's messages are different from anything they have ever heard before in a church.

We decided to begin with a book of prayers. What follows is a collection of fifty-two, most of which come from the last twenty years of Fred's services. They are reconstructed from the original scratched-out and margin-filled drafts, with some updating, rewording, and deleting (including many personal references to people in the congregation or the Warren Wilson community). Editing was a group effort, with Fred doing the major first-round alterations.

As we searched for a way to organize the book, several recurring themes emerged: being thankful, opening the senses, asking forgiveness, living life fully, being aware of human limitations *and* abilities. Yet we resisted the notion of lumping the prayers together by subject or theme, keeping in mind those who would read them straight through and might prefer a more interesting, varied path.

Finally, something should be said about style and format. Just as Fred Ohler searches in these prayers for the meaning of the Word, so does he explore the meanings of the words. Often the result is more poetic than typically prayerlike. Having grown up during radio days, spending after-school hours listening to good stories artfully read, he has developed a marvelous reading voice and ability. Using both, he has the uncanny knack of making the words easily understood and the deeper meanings clear. He reads slowly, at ease enough to pause and savor along the way. Sometimes he groups words together in an unusual manner. His pacing is just right, just irregular enough to avoid monotony. Often he puts the emphasis in unexpected places, choosing to illuminate a normally overlooked word, one that is usually prayed without thinking. Sometimes he will divide up clichéd words in search of their original, fresh meanings ("re - creation," "all - ways").

Instead of condensing his words into a standard form, we have tried to preserve his unique style of reading within the printed text. Vocal emphasis has translated into capitalization; words typically whole are divided and explored with hyphens; wide spaces represent pauses, as do the unpunctuated ends of lines (in lieu of commas). We hope the chosen format allows the spoken rhythm to be felt, and one man's way of speaking to God to be heard and read.

Lisa A. Ohler and
Beverly Hummel Ohler, editors

Author's Note

I am deeply grateful to the people of the Warren Wilson community; they have ministered to me and been my friends. I am indebted to Catherine Clark and Clay Berry, who helped so much with typing and word processing; to Louis Miles and John Koegel, for their good counsel; to Marion Shepherd Weeks, for her reference wizardry; and to Harold L. Twiss and the editors at Westminister/John Knox Press, for their prompt, patient, and careful shepherding.

Most of all I thank my daughters, Lisa and Chrisann, and my wife, Beverly. Without them this book would not have been.

Better Than Nice
and Other
Unconventional Prayers

A Chorus Beyond Hallelujah

Creative God
the cosmos worships
cleanly
consistently
constantly—
amoebae halve
electron and proton mate
planets pirouette in orbit—
a million atoms in our fingernails
and each one
is
a microcosm
a miniature galaxy!

The animals worship
cleanly
consistently
constantly—
the flight of a butterfly is "plashless" praise
blackbird's song is a psalm
tiger's grace   antelope's flight   gator's grin   worm's wiggle
attest to your deft touch.
They worship You by being what they are—
each a mystery
all a miracle
in their balance   variety   complexity   being.
Were no human animal
ever to pray
You would be abundantly praised.
The birthing   growing   living   dying
grace
beauty
struggle of all the creatures
is a chorus beyond
Hallelujah
and we delude ourselves into imagining that
there would be no life without us
no worship without OUR hymns.

May we join in?
Will we?
We can choose to praise
or curse

or yawn
with the breath of life in us
and that makes it matter.
In creation's chorus
still listen
for our small voice
hear our simple song
and note our part

amen.

A God Worthy of Our Needs

We are
incurably
strangely
persistently worshiping creatures.
She loves Prince Charming
he is weak with awe before his mirror
one idolizes her father
another adores his car.
We mock old idols
and idolize new gods;
we dabble in divinities
but, prodigal, return home
to have no other gods beside
Us.

Reform
inform
our deformed worship.
End the tyranny of gods who lie
fail
crash
melt
beginning with our tiny inflated egos;
liberate us to You
God
worthy of our needs
Being up to our love

amen.

A Pettiness of Massive Consequence

Merciful God
please forgive
all those little moments
the tawdry times
when we have a mean spirit
a paltry soul
a pettiness of massive consequence to expiate.
We hear the gossip
our conscience resists
we almost challenge the game
but play along
add the morsel we heard in the market
the tidbit we picked up on the phone
the cliché we remember in our grandmother's voice
something prejudiced
ignorant
cruel.
We want to speak up
defend another color
an absent friend
a whole people
but we bite our tongue and say nothing
and grin at the unfunny joke
and capitulate.

Expiate our pettiness
every paltry
vulgar
mean act
lest we miss our chance
the next time
forever

amen.

A Way to Go

God of unceasing change
hear the gasps of those who are
stuck
trapped
addicted
perpetually adolescent
prematurely resigned
thinking that it will never get any better
clearer
or gentler for them.
Whisper . . .
thunder!
But do get through to them with the saving word
that persons need not stay the way they are.

Hear also the anxious, unspoken fears
of those who are productive
successful
comfortable
finding satisfaction in their work
pleasure in life
love at home
You in your heaven and all right with their world.
They never step on the sidewalk cracks
they say their prayers
they see their children beautifully, peacefully asleep in bed
and want so much to stop time
that
this innocence, security, and safety may be preserved forever.
Speak to them the saving word
the strange good news
that persons will not stay the way they are.

The word of faith is the same for us all:
we are always unfinished;
You are not through with us yet.
In the painful and pleasant changes of life
we meet You
and the Christ.
We call Him the Way and mean only the destination;
He is also and especially the journey
the process
the getting there

within   amid   through
the heart attack, the conversion, the birth, the death
the growing up and growing old and becoming like a child.
Good news to her who is not as lost as she thinks.
Good news to him who is not as saved as he imagines.
Good news to us all.
Way to go

amen.

When There Is No Peace

We ARE pro peace, Lord;
You DO understand that?
It's on our agenda;
You can't expect us to do EVERYTHING
can You?
There are other issues
and we do what we can—
pressure our politicians
pray politely
and think good thoughts.

Prince of Peace
what will it take for us to choke
as we prepare to spend
trillions of dollars for "defense"
millions every hour offensively?
Lord of Love
what will it take for us to shudder
as we prepare to kill "for Christ's sake"?

War and death flare across our screens
live by satellite.
We see it all
and none of it registers;
our lips say
"It could all end in the incineration of the earth—today"
and our hearts do not know
or feel
or care.

What will it take
to make us gasp for breath
gulp for air
ache for all we're worth
for a just and costly and authentic peace?
Whatever it takes
give us

amen.

be (bē) *intr.v.* 1. To exist in actuality; have reality; am. 2. To exist in a specified place: *England,| Now that April's there* occupy a specified position: *The place; occur.* 5. To go. *Used* tenses: *Have you ever been t* befall. Used in the subjunctiv copula linking a subject and or pronoun, in such senses

As Good as Your Word

God
good God
good Word
Yahweh
I AM
living, active
Being verb—
we have reduced You to a noun
a being
a word
subject made object that we can control.
Your Word is open
our ears are closed
or distracted to death
barraged by words of ad garble
psycho-babble
Tower of Babel.
Your Word is creative
("Let there be"—and it is—and it is good—it is very good).
Your Word is enfleshed
(in His being and saying and doing and dying and rising
truth before us, grace in person).
In our beginning
is Your Word
Being made flesh.
May we be
as good
as Your Word

amen.

At Least Forever

Limitless God
we live in a time of transience
disposing people in a throwaway culture.
We produce   consume   use up   cast off
things
persons
You.
We too
are haunted by
the new absolute of ever-new experience;
we too
fear deep down
that people can be fathomed
that we'll say, "Is that all there is?"
We confess
that we have treated others and You
like crossword puzzles—
intriguing when blank   useless when filled in.
What good is a solved crossword puzzle?

Forgive us
and help us to see
that nothing is simple.
Who of us understands a cat?
Who of us totally understands our best friend
our dearest love   our own self
You?
How long would it take to solve
the puzzle of their personalities
the mystery of Your reality?
Forever?
At least.

Shame on our presumption
forgiveness on our arrogance.
Help us to rediscover a healthy sense of curiosity
an honest humility
an openness to surprise   and joy
in the presence of all mysteries
from the amoeba
to You

amen.

A Rose in Winter

We pray for life in the womb
for the child soon to be born
wanted / unwanted
legitimate / illegitimate
healthy / flawed
born / stillborn
still   born
birthed in satin / born in the streets.

We pray for Him who is all children
wanted / unwanted.

And we pray
for a rose
in winter

amen.

Better Fears

O God
it is so easy
to be afraid
to be made afraid.

Demagogues of every sort
have always counted on our fears
to scare us into submission.

Politicians and preachers
commissars and evangelists
make people afraid—
afraid of what will happen to them
afraid of death
and therefore of life
afraid of differences
strangers
joy.

The fearmongers are so successful
because they find in us
such willing subjects.

But the gospel of perfect love
comes to us
to cast out fear—
from our beginning.

Some of us
have never affirmed
our first birth—
have never said "Good!" to our emergence
"Very good!" to our creation.
Be midwife to our self-respect
and mother to our growth.

Perfect love
will cast out fear
and when You are through with us
we will be fearless.
In the mean time
at least help us
to move from petty fears
to better ones;
from fears of hell

to admissions of joylessness;
from quaking before opinions and modes and fashions
to fearing
loss of our integrity
and untruth in our very souls.

We would say "Bravo!"
to
our birth
our re - birth
Your will that created us
our choice to be
and to become

amen.

Better to Have Loved

Passionate Lord
we naturally
understandably
prudently prefer the wisdom of the Buddha, who said
"He who loves fifty has fifty woes,
who loves none has no woe . . ."
for it hurts to care
to extend
to let other lives matter
because they suffer
and they fail
and they die
and we'd rather not hurt so
but we are haunted
by Your holy Fool
who cried over Jerusalem
and wept for Lazarus
who feels each pain
and every body's aches
who suffered about
with
for
all
and loves every soul
as if it were his own child.
We have much to repent
more to learn
most to feel
for Christ's sake

amen.

Better Than Nice

"Thank you for a nice evening—
we must do it again, sometime."
"Thanks for the present—it was very nice."
"Sincerely yours . . ."
"Thank You, God, for health, for life, for whatever . . . amen."

O God, who of us does not mouth such
kempt
precedented
underwhelming gratuities?
Who of us doesn't sense how very shallow they are?
For even we
have known those moments
those shining experiences
when gratitude was not a stifling obligation
but an ecstatic necessity
a joy
a delight
when our very souls were grateful
to be alive
to learn
to love
to wonder
to say, "AH!"

lleluia

On Tuesday
the sun can shine, everything go well
and we can be bitter
angry
frustrated
and sour;
on the very next day
amid the rain and the troubles and the garbage of a bad Wednesday
we find ourselves strangely appreciative . . .
same world—different soul.
The problem lies within us
and not out in the stars
or in the phase of the moon.
But what makes the difference
between
the bitterness of hell
and the blessing of gratitude?

O God
what can we conceive?
What must we perceive?
What is the secret sense?

amen.

Blessed Untime

Thank You, God, for
the amazing gift of sleep . . .
such a quiet
overlooked
good and gentle grace it is.
Sleep:
blessed untime
bath of un - consciousness
pain's easing balm
doing all death's duties
but the kill.

He cannot sleep enough;
she resents every minute lost to work and ambition.
The escapist sleeps, mindless;
the insomniac tosses, mind - full.
We praise You for the helpless hours
when all snore
and none is ugly
when our private myths have their dress rehearsals . . .
the crippled
walk
the blind
see
an old woman
is a Fräulein again
and no one
sleeps alone.
And AH
we rise from the dead
born again
re - created to this never-before
nor-ever-again
day . . .
new
and fresh
and Yours

amen.

By Our Love

By our love, Lord, by our love
not by creed
or propriety
wisdom
or style
nor what we say
nor how we seem . . .
by our love.
That's all
that's enough
that's Christ's one spirit
to touch
to care
to break out of the petty prison
of the ego's cell
to stand up for our sister
cry with our brother
sing with our neighbor.
More love, Lord
more love
and the praise be Yours

amen.

Constant Change

Constant God
dis - illusion us of the siren notion
that change alone will do it.
Take from our souls
the great American lie
that life is always somewhere else up ahead
that somehow a new place
the next time
a new love
a new god
tomorrow's experience
will do it.
Help us to accept the fact that everywhere we go
there we are.
Help us to celebrate the truth
that unless it is well in our soul
it is no good
any   where
any   time.

Surprising God
dis - illusion us of the stolid notion
that change can be forbidden
that we can freeze time
eternalize place
or suspend animation.
Who of us has not wanted to stop the flow, the parting
the death of a sister
the loss of a friend
the growth of a person?
How we love to turn tents into cathedrals
transfigurations into booths
loves into possessions
and homes into museums
but Your love is out ahead calling for courage
resurrection
risk.

O God, it's not too hard to love a being
and be comfortable
but people aren't beings   they're becomings
and it's hard to love a becoming.
It hurts

it tears at our unfaith.
It's hard to love a becoming
unless we, too, by Your constant surprising
are also becoming
who we are.
Becoming God
proceed, we pray

amen.

Feast Yourselves

God beyond all our gods
Lord of lords
You offer us life's bread
crusty   warm   yeasty   buttered   dark—
as healthful as good—
and we gum day-old white;
in the midst of Your banquet
we nibble away
at the same
old
American cheese sandwich.
There is kielbasa to savor
there are tongues to speak
Kilimanjaros to scale
shells to shed
lives to live.

Lure us to
worlds richer than our world
selves deeper than our egos
other selves (within us and without us).
Woo us until
"my" means participation, not possession
"my own" means belonging, not exclusion
and each of us
joins all of us
at Your exuberant party.
Please pass the wine

amen.

Except We Become

"Mirror, mirror, on the wall
who's the fairest of them all?"
And You give us a telescope
to look through from the wrong end.
Who is the greatest in Your kingdom?
Christ puts a child into our midst saying to us that
to receive a child into the fortress of our lives
is to receive Him.
And
unless we turn   turn   turn
and become childlike
we have grown down
not up.
Help us, God, to not ignore those whose angels watch Your face
to not discount them
or patronize
or force-feed
or push them too soon into adulthood
or fear them—
for more of us fear children
than we can ever admit.

Thank You, God
for their honest pride, ravenous curiosity, unspoiled mysticism
and
the memories   dreams   hopes   innocence
they stir in us.
Thank You for
storybooks
and fantasy
for Dorothy and Dumbo
Jiminy Cricket and Pooh Bear.

> An elephant is flying
> a cricket me-o-mying
> rhinoceri are sighing
> hyenae are a'crying.

> Strangely, on the one hand,
> Dorothy lives in Wonderland;
> oddly, on the other hand,
> Alice visits Kansas.

Give us the great good sense
to cast aside
our jaded sophistication
our world-weary "adulthood"
our left-brained unwonder
that we may with all God's children
see that
"Morning has broken like the FIRST morning."
Thank You, God, for "Eden's play" today
for recreation, re - creation
wonderful   wonderful   wonder - full world

amen.

I Dis - Believe; Help My Belief

En - able us
mercy - full God
to confess   and repent of   our sins—
not just the itsy-bitsy ones
but the great one   the root fault
our atheism.

We're not asking forgiveness for our questions
the honest "why?" in the face of death
the "why?" in the midst of great injustice
the Job
the Jeremiah
the Jesus in us feeling sometimes God - forsaken.
We're not asking forgiveness for the "atheism" of dis - believing
a doctrine   a system   somebody else's answer
anybody's false god.

But we are asking forgiveness for the real atheism of
our superficiality
our skimming along
our ordered utopias
our terrible craving for safety
our trivial religiosity
our preference for religion over faith
for law over gospel.
The fast which You want
is not to boast of our humility
but to liberate the prisoner
to "break every yoke"
to have compassion
for that sad little person
who needs our love—
who is ourselves.

Love us
shake us
lure us to the gaps
to where it is more dangerous
and bitter
and extravagant
and bright—
to where Your glory flashes

amen.

Extraordinary Moments / Ordinary Lives

Thank You, God
for powerless people in broad daylight facing tanks
with dignity
and élan
and nothing much more . . .
for the magnitude of beauty
emanating from those once-in-a-lifetime moments
when the impossible is done with panache . . .
for those bright   burning   meteoric moments
in lives (even ours)—
moments of flair and surprise
when a meek man finds sudden courage
a fearful woman bursts forth in an aria
and a shooting star lights the sky.

And thank You, God
for the other side of life . . .
the patient   dependable   homely
life-giving courage
of people
we can   and have   and will depend on
who live for more than the moment
whose goodness grows like a tree   (slow   steady   rooted)
in season and out
who have that weathered, promises-kept beauty of many days.
We owe them our very lives;
we owe You our thanks for them;
we owe ourselves no less.

Whether by sudden heroism
or solid integrity
grant us the courage and the patience
to live

amen.

Extravagant God

Excessive
generous
lavish God . . .
why do You waste so much time on us?
You create rainbows
that no one sees;
shower down intricate   separate   unique
stunning
snowflakes by the billions
and one at a time
that we greet not with applause
but with complaints of inconvenience.
You place whales
beneath fathoms of ocean
singing their plaintive
haunting songs
too deep
for our ears
to hear.
You create fantastic jungles within a square foot of grass
a universe in an atom
breathtaking places that have never been seen or appreciated
by a single human being—
not ever.
Why is Your kindness so extravagant
Your excess so much—
why are we so bored and dull?
Why do we appreciate water most in a desert
health only during sickness
our friend when he leaves
our love when she dies?
Should we pray for less
for You to ration Your grace
to waste no rainbow?

Forgive us.
You don't paint rainbows just for us to see
nor make birdsong just for us to hear.
Rebuke our terrible pride
and chastise our deism
that imagines You created only once
long ago

and can't perceive Genesis now
or Eden here
or what a new day means.
Help us to do two impossible things:
to take it ALL in
(every miraculous atom of it)
and
to waste our time on A rose
a place
a time
a person.
Perhaps one   will bring us to all
full time   to eternity
one blackbird   to You.
Prodigal God, may we find
a millionth of the joy that clearly is Yours

amen.

Good and Gentle Grace

O God, we want to sing You a new song
to be glad in You
to enjoy You—
to be moved
to feel
not to be bored to death
but to be excited to life.

Thank You for peace
and salvation
and today
just for today—
for all the gifts we overlook
that bear us grace - fully along:
for a night's sleep
when body and soul can rest
and trust Your world to go on without us.

Thank You, God, for water that woke us up
for toothpaste that sweetened morning mouth
for the good lingering smell of soap
for getting the curlers out and the whiskers off
for the newspaper early there and the mail, late and urgent
for clothes on our back and warmth in our home
for cucumbers that are cool
and loves that are not
for our underwhelming merit
and Your overwhelming grace—
gift - ed
talent - ed
and en - abled.

We sing our appreciation—
for Eli Whitney
and Mahatma Gandhi
for Sarah and Abraham
and Eve and Adam
and all the overlooked saints and creators in our midst
for the uncountable fullness of Your providence
and for Your constancy.
We thank You
for this freely given day

amen.

Never Fail, Never Succeed

Speak, Lord
Your disturbing
unwanted
off-balance
necessary word
to every Libra
each timid
safe
and sorry soul.
Speak Your prophetic word
afflict the complacent
discomfort those
who are unwilling to get their hands soiled
or their faith ruffled
or their lives lived
who would rather withdraw passing than fail
who by never failing, never succeed.
Give them
less the Boss, more Zorba
less Thomas, more Peter
less of Tetzel, more of Luther
Jeremiah, not Leviticus
Jesus, not Moses
cold or hot, not tepid.

And when they—
no, we—are done
grant that
our lives
flawed
sinful
doubt - full
dauntless and faithed
will be lived, not hedged.
We pray
in the name of Him
who is the Life
who held nothing back

amen.

Real

Beautiful God
how good it is
that we have seen
in the midst of all the gray and banal
and sad stuff of life
a person
really caring about truth
that we have seen something so beautiful
it took our boredom away—
quiet courage in a timid person
a man who could laugh at himself
a genuinely humble person who didn't know she was humble
(and whom to tell would ruin it)
real indignation that was better than self-righteousness
or silence.
We have seen love
in other people
and even in ourselves.
Breathe on
that glow
that it may not die
but burn more brightly
clearly
often

amen.

From Breakfast to the Eschaton

O living God
we are alive
glad to BE alive
and we try to be life-affirming
to fight death in all its forms and faces
to oppose war
make peace
honor the environment
choose life.

Help us to see the paradox
the complexity
the depth of our debt
for each of us lives off the lives of others.
Our life is possible
only because other life has died.
We would hide from that
and put the abattoir on the other side of town
and the farmer at a romantic distance
hide the dying in plastic
and packages
and processing.
We should know
that today's cow is tomorrow's meal
that living wheat is grimly reaped for our bread
that broccoli is killed to grace our plate
that flowers are picked for our weddings
that animals
and plants
and human beings have died
that we may live. . . .
From breakfast to the eschaton
our lives are good
growing
alive
possible
because of the vicarious sacrifice of life in all its forms
from cotton to Christ.
Such is our debt;
such is Your grace.
Our grace
must transcend wooden words at table

must be better than verbiage
will be as good as our word—
a promise
that all that dying for us
shall not be wasted.
So be it

amen.

Awe - full

Great and holy God
awe and reverence
fear and trembling
do not come easily to us
for we are not
Old Testament Jews
or Moses
or mystics
or sensitive enough.
Forgive us
for slouching into Your presence
with little expectation
and less awe
than we would eagerly give a visiting dignitary.
We need
neither Jehovah nor a buddy—
neither "the Great and Powerful Oz" nor "the man upstairs."
Help us
to want what we need . . .
You
God
and may the altar of our hearts
tremble with delight
at
Your visitation

amen.

I Want a Miracle

O God
I want a miracle—
a clear
unequivocal
inescapable sign—
a thing I cannot explain
a proof I cannot debate
an earnest of Your existence
and my faith.
Why do You not act?
I want a miracle—
not a baby born well and normal
not a sunrise seen
not a rain's whisper heard
but a REAL miracle.
I WANT a miracle
I . . .

My God how I need Your forgiveness of my presumption
arrogance
unfaith
death
for the dimness and numbness of my soul.
There are those who see the skies open
and explain it away;
there are others who see the common uncommonly
and under - stand.

I will promise to do what I can
to wake up and come alive
to take time
and risk solitude
to hear a tree
see a poem
swim in the rain
look INTO her eyes
to REALLY see and hear and feel
even a tiny portion of
the million mysteries
the constant magic that is
afoot . . .
and underfoot

and all around
and all within.

O God
take the sleepers from my eyes
the wax from my ears
the cataracts from my soul.
I need the gift of Your spirit
Your Holy Spirit
to bring clarity to my perception
joy to my heart
and eternity to my daily round

amen.

No Chicken Soup That Is Not Consecrated

Lord
thank You
for a day to desist
to cease
to rest
to catch our soul's breath
a Sabbath not of blue laws and ruly behavior
but of freedom   and color   and joy.
this IS the day which You have made
not just another day, one more day, day after day
but a new day, the only day, a holyday.
In a world where there is
no chicken soup that is not consecrated
no ground that is un - holy
no ordinary that is not extra—
where we are all ways up to our eyes in miracles
but most times blind as moles—
grant us the good sense
to see and to savor
the eternity of this day

amen.

Incarnation

O God
perhaps
all time is good time
every place a good place;
perhaps
we should be no respecters of time or space
each day a Christmas
and every field a church.
But
we're not made that way.
If each day were Christmas
Christ would not be specially born.
If every place were holy
nowhere would be special
historical
located
particular
unique.
Therefore
we acknowledge our need for rhythms in our life
for epiphanies of time:
birthdays
recollections of death
anniversaries of joy
commencements and graduations
baptisms and bar mitzvahs
the first time we knew Eros
the last time we saw Paris
right time
full time
in time
and
timely.

We acknowledge our need for places "just right"
for theophanies of space:
a tree house
a sanctuary
some sacred grove
the cloistered attic
a secluded den

Jerusalem
home.

Grant that
today
may be a good time
and
here
may be
the Sabbath of location
through Christ our Lord
who is every where always
only because
He was some where
once

amen.

Life Is God-Sized

We bring our idols;
You are God.
We come with our theologies;
You are "God only wise."
We keep trying to reduce life to size
with our theology
our biology
our psychology
with all our ologies . . .
and
You elude our logic
You burst our boxes.
For that we praise You
and rejoice
that life is God-sized
never fully understood
drenched in mysteries
more startling than all our systems.

Humble us all
lest we shrink Your world to what WE know
or can handle.
Help us each
to let it be as unruly
wild
and grace - full
as it is.
Loosen us
to dance with joy
and wail with sorrow
to laugh   to cry   to celebrate   to grieve.
Help us
not only to be caught by the exceptional
but to be stunned by the ordinary
to marvel at what we call "common"—
sparrow
the people
sense
touch
and all the small and daily blessings.
My God
how incredible that we are here (and not a million OTHER places)

that we are together
that we are alive
that we are at all.
Keep us
young expectant unsure open
nervous sensitive
and alive . . .
at whatever age

amen.

No Accounting

Good God—we give thanks!
for things great and small
public and private
tender and thund'rous
for the "splendor in the grass"
and the space between the stars
for health and healing
and muscles and minds
for the masculinity of men
and the femininity of women
for the converse in each
and Your image in both
for the innocent smoothness of babies
and the wrinkled wisdom of old people
for growing up and going back
for forgetting and remembering
for leaving home to find home
for every borrowed atom of our bodies
and every unearned ounce of Your grace
good God—we give thanks.

We confess our thanks
for our gratitude is selfish, our appreciation superficial;
we calculate blessings, tally kindnesses.
We make of Your good graces means to our ends
unable to welcome beauty just because it is beautiful
unable to greet knowledge simply because it is true
unable to embrace goodness as its own reward
without praise or advancement or medals.
How often we have loved You as a means to our ends
when we were frightened   or lonely   or desperate
because we feared hell
or craved heaven.
We have loved You to get rewarded—
loving You is reward enough.

Help us to leave behind bargains and deals
scratching that we may be scratched
loving that we may be loved
giving that we may receive
our left hand knowing all too soon and all too well
what our right hand is about.

Good God—we give You
thanks
for You

amen.

When All Heaven Breaks Loose

Lord, when we are weak
we pray without urging (if not without ceasing).
When she is stricken with cancer
or our foundation crumbles
when we are scared
shattered
sad
or things dis - integrate
we cry out for Your help.
For that we are not ashamed;
we have no regret.

But when we are strong
when it's summertime and life is easy
when all's right with our world and You're safely in heaven
when we have that sense of well-being
Lord, do not let us be
but turn our seeming strength into gratitude
our well-being into thanks - giving
and our recreation into re - creation.
In winter and in summer
no less when pride seduces than when despair overwhelms
when we collapse
and when all heaven breaks loose
when we are weak
and when we are not
Lord, leave us not
to our own defenses

amen.

Nobody's Puppet

O God
who speaks for us?
What dead hand of the past ties our tongue?
Why are the sins of our forebears
visited upon us
and on our children's children?
We live off the past—
its glories as well as its limits—
so
who are we that are living, speaking?
If we swallow all those little old men and women
are they assimilated?
digested?
exorcised?
or festering within like some incipient ulcer?

We try to cut it out.
And when we try
launch forth
become who we are
they urge us to stay within the lines
to paint grass green
and the one time they like our picture
and say
"That's good—
that's REALLY good!" . . .
they've got it—
us—
downside-up.

O God, what's the use?
How sad
how very sad
to have others live our lives for us
to have had excused absences from our own living
to miss our best years
and be strangers to ourselves.
Do make THAT seem more frightful
than the judgments from the grave
or the misunderstandings of parent, teacher, or friend.

Better yet
help us to prefer being Edgar Bergen

to Charlie McCarthy
a person
not a ventriloquist's dummy
and to love who
and whose
we are

amen.

None So Blind

We close our eyes, Lord
that we may see
for when we stare
we are like two glazed mirrors before each other
bouncing reflection off reflection off images.
Place before us a face
the face of one we hate
to see past the mask we have placed there
to the sadness
the lines
the eyes;
place before us
the face of the one we love most and see least (to see anew
the look that took all breath away)
the face of a dead father that keeps going blank (dear God
how could we forget?).

It's easy to look away
to avert our gaze;
it's easy to stare
in some kind of "you'll look away before I do" contest
(it's not hard if we focus on the forehead
or look through
or past
or over).
But to see
the face
the eyes
the soul behind the eyes
and
another seeing us . . .
O
O my
O my God
we see;
cure our blindness

amen.

Owning Up

O God, it is easy to pray for "mankind" and "the world"
to anguish about the great problems
to confess humanity's faults
global sins
international stupidities.
It is costless to confess my sins
if I keep my prayer comfortably vague
piously general
if I never get closer than
"We have all sinned and fallen short of Your glory."

Help me to confess
only that sin which I have committed
which I honestly would get off my soul's back
for which I am responsible
refusing the easy alibis of original sin
Freudian determinism
or "The Devil made me do it."
I don't know if the world has lied—
I have lied.
I don't know if the world has conspired against love—
I have conspired against love.
I have hated
I have killed
and
I have tried to come clean
to own up
to quit faking it.

Give me Your answer
not in the easy absolution of assured pardon
but later today
and tomorrow
in the fabric of my changing life.
I don't want cheap grace;
I do pray for Your costly mercy
for Christ's sake

amen.

Not for Granted

My God, what a morning!
Thank You for light
bright
warm
speckled
color - full
new / good / this
day.
Help us to take it
not FOR granted
but AS granted;
open our eyes
to this season
to every season
to winter
storm
suffering
ice.

We thank You
that life is not easy
that it costs and matters
that joy and faith are possible
in season and out.

We are delight - ed that You are God enough for all of life—
for all its serious / funny
tragic / comic
up / down
in / out variety.
We are glad for change
for fresh winds blowing
for Your good Spirit stirring
here / there / every   where.

And we are glad that some things DON'T change
like the seasons
growing up / growing old
the need for love
the church's maligned / inadequate / good service
Christ's persistent love
Your incredible patience
friends to be needed

children and grandchildren to be worried over
work to be done
wounds to be healed
ignorance to be outgrown
truth to be discovered
death to be overcome.

Deliver us, O God, from past worship, present apathy, future shock.
You have given us the birthday gift of this day;
we give You the weak and fragile gift of our gratitude.
It is too little, too flawed
but it is OUR gift.
Please take it—
for our soul's sake

amen.

The Sun Belongs to No Nation

Thank You, God
for the dependability
and the democracy
of nature.
We are glad:
that the wind blows
across the fences
and the boundaries
whether carrying fresh air
or pollution;
that the sun belongs to no nation;
that from a satellite the national boundaries
and DMZs
and Berlin walls
are invisible;
that
the pink
and green
and red
and blue nations of the map
are all earth-colored.
We applaud:
that the mouse visits rich and poor alike;
that it's possible for the suited and the unsuited
to be children in the sun;
that Your nature spills over all our limits
light -ly
gracious - ly
persistent - ly.
Thank You
for coloring outside the lines

amen.

Providence

God of our life—
God of all our becoming
winding
helical
hope - full
fear - full years—
we praise You in retrospect.
When we look back
through all our deciding   planning   wishing
through doors opened
at doors closed
best-laid plans
and worst-kept secrets
how can we deny Your providence and grace
at work in the fabric of our lives?
Even allowing for our great gifts of rationalization
and special pleading
how can we look back
and not see
haunting traces of Your grace?
We can.
We do.
We praise.

Why
can we not see that Your beguiling hand
is present
and in prospect?
We ask no road map
no life-back guarantees
no inoculation against suffering.
But when we are hurting
and pain floods all our vision
grant us faith.
When we are strong
(especially when we are strong)
grant us faith—
a daring
willing-to-be-surprised
trust in Your provident plan for each special life
even ours

amen.

Remember Mama, Papa

Mother and Father of us all
Parent of all people
Source of life
and love
and caring
we remember Mama   Mutti   Mom
the one You chose to conceive
and bear
to birth
and bear with us
the mother in whom
through whom
by whom
You graced us into life;
we remember and appreciate her. . . .

Father and Mother of us all
Parent of all people
Source of life
and love
and caring
we remember Papa   Padre   Pop
the one You chose to impregnate
and stand by
to support
and nurture us
the father in whom
through whom
by whom
You graced us into life;
we remember and appreciate him. . . .

O Parent of all people
we salute the hearts of ALL parents
mothers
fathers
grandparents   godparents   stepparents
substitute mothers   surrogate fathers
the unmarried
the childless who care about and love
children with different genes.

Help them all—help us—
to know what to grant
and what to deny
when to say yes
and when no is love's best word
when to intervene
and when to stand clear.
Help them—help us—
to love enough to be childlike
in wonder
in trust
in the capacity to be surprised
and the ability to be delighted.
Help them and help us
to love enough to surrender children
to the larger claims of life
to the family extended into all eternity.

O God, Genesis of us all
Parent of all people
we pray for all parents
through Your child
Jesus Christ our Lord

amen.

Saying Grace

Grace we say at meals;
"Amazing Grace" we sing at worship;
and grace it is, gracious God.
By the frown of Your grace we are judged;
by the laughter of Your grace we are saved;
grace relieves the fear in our hearts which it taught our hearts.
By grace
we are gifted to life
we are saved from our works
we are alive at all.
Is any one not indebted, dependent, blessed beyond belief?
Who of us thought our selves up?
Which of us is self-conceived?
Why do we act as though we have no belly buttons
and imagine that we are isolate, unconnected?

Help us to contemplate our navels
remember the cord
celebrate the ties that bind and the love that liberates.
Just as we are, "without one plea"
unjust as we are, with a thousand excuses—
dependent as heaven
and ungrateful as hell—
we say "grace"
Your grace we see.
Even that
is a gift

amen.

The Fifth Season

For four seasons
and all the cycles
within us and without us
for periods, tides, phases
for birth and growth and decline and death
thank You, God.
To live is to have rhythm
and time is the signature on all Your compositions.

Forgive us that
too often we fight against the rhythm
trying to be twenty when we're fifty
craving adulthood when we're still children
coveting summer when it's winter
detesting the heat when it's July
too often unwilling
to let go and let You be
in Your good time.

Forgive us no less when we worship Chronos
cower before clocks
schedule surprises
and tick our lives to death.

We are not Canaanites, we are Christians
and for us there is a fifth season.
You became flesh
that flesh might become You.
Love invaded time
and love is the fifth season
not bound by daylight time
or standard time
or Pacific time
or troubled time
or any time
always seasoned, always seasoning
as old as "in the beginning"
as permanent as forever
as new
as now
as possible as Christ.
Make him possible in us

amen.

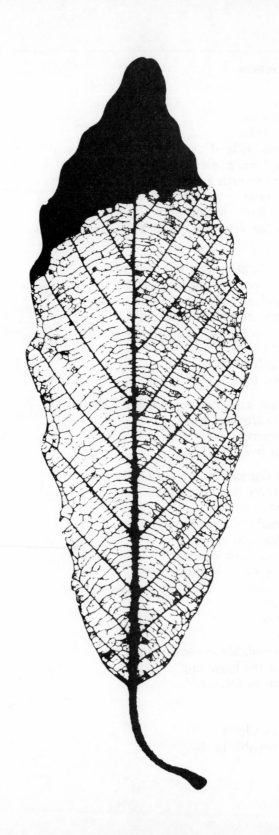

Second Sight

Eye of God
how little we see
how much we overlook.
What we take in we miss;
whom we figure out, we kill
with a familiarity which births contempt
or worse . . . boredom.
God, give us the eyes of St. Francis—
to see our enemy as a person—
to imagine him crying
or praying
or asleep.
God, give us Jesus' eyes—
to see
inside
what might have been
what yet can be
even in
especially in
those we think we know best.
When we make them in our image
we play god poorly.

Enlighten us to expect peaches from pits
Christ from babies
genius from friends
and saints from selves.

Lighten us to have
the imagination
insight
and good sense
to "vision them into splendor"

amen.

The Tribute of Candor

We worship You;
we honor the saints.
Help us to admit
and then to celebrate
that they were not plaster
but flesh.
With the tribute of candor
we acknowledge:
David's lust and violence
Mary's overprotective love of her boy
Paul's self-hate and mitigated arrogance
Francis's proud humility
Martin's gross crudeness and fierce rage.
With all the saints, they were human
beings
whose greatness is greater when we appreciate
their sins
their struggles
their victories
and our kinship.
Help us to demythologize our fathers and mothers
to honor who they truly are, not to idolize some poor perfection
that we may become the saints we already are
in Your sight

amen.

Waiting

O Wisdom
knowing what we know—
we believe;
knowing what we don't know—
we wait.
We wait like
a wife on a widow's walk
a child on the day before Christmas
a father worrying at the window late at night
a mother ten months pregnant
like hostages   captives   Babylonian Jews.
The more we know
the more we know we don't know
and our overstanding gives way to
mystery
humility
anticipation
patience
and advent

amen.

The Fullness Thereof

The earth is YOURS, Lord
and the fullness thereof—the FULLness!
The earth IS Yours
full of height
(help us to rise and soar
to look back on this small blue spaceship
and out into space—
past our system, our galaxy, to the atom).
The earth IS Yours
full of depth
(help us to go down—to see within one dandelion
its tiny parachutes
wee green blades, hardy root, the very universe
and its indomitable Christ).
The earth IS Yours
full of beauty
(the greatest art in the universe is there in a fly's eye
a butterfly's shingled wings
an old woman's wrinkled face
an - other human being).
The earth IS Yours
full of ecstasy
(exaltation and depth
joy and sorrow
real hearts greatly broken
true loves really lost
and death's worst efforts   faced
gone through   undergone
overcome).

Forgive us
when we desecrate Your infinite
startling
awe - full
awesome
mysterious creation.
Forgive us
the real atheism
of living on the surface
skimming along
overlooking
or just getting by.

Judge us whenever we say "It's ONLY an animal"
or "Oh, I know him"
or "Is that all there is?"
or "BORing. . . ."

Good God, what a world!
Passion birthed it
Your love sustains it all
from speck
to sun
to soul.
And only when we feel and see and sense the fullness thereof
just as we appreciate Your gift with interest
do we
can we
shall we know the earth
and the earth's Lord
and ours

amen.

The Son Also Rises (A Prayer for Easter)

Lord, no Easter ever celebrated a world without death
and this day is no exception.
In the world
in our community
in our souls—
while we live we are always being given up to death. . . .
Never the less
closer to finally
how ever
Christ's resurrection prevails
and therefore we cry out
"L'chayim!"—To life!—
that in - credible
in - soluble
un - stoppable mystery
which is Yours to give
and ours to live.

Lord, we are grateful
that
seedtime and harvest
cold and heat
summer and winter
day and night will not cease
that
every rainbow is a covenant
and every sunrise a promise.

Lord, we are grateful
that
floods clap their hands
and hills sing for joy
and what the birds do by nature we may do by choice—
to sing   to sing   to sing!

Lord, we are grateful
for
despair that is in vain and labor that is not
work that is worship and worship that is play
being part of a world that includes April
a species that produced Bach
and a century that birthed our sister, Teresa.

Lord, we are grateful for the ubiquity of life
and the democracy of death
which none may evade (like taxes)
nor any buy off (like justice)
nor slaughter (like the innocents)
but which all must face
for life to come true and belief to be real
for choice to count and love to matter.

Thank You, God
that
in a world where "little men cast long shadows
because the sun is setting"
the Son also rises
and all the naked emperors
and massive egos
and fakes
dry up
and gentle Christ rises lovingly from the grave
worthy of praise
for
His grace - full entry
His limitless love
His absolute conquest of death
and His unremitting affirmation of life.
He is mighty because of His honor
great because of His goodness
and alive because He loves.
Therefore we praise Him and call Him Lord

amen.

Tourist Eyes

Lord
we're at home
amid old familiar places
faces
lives
somewhat at ease in Zion
lulled
by the illusion
of familiar forever.

Tip us off balance.
Etch in our souls
the absolute truth
that we are all
pilgrims
sojourners
tourists.

We take it all for granted
overlook what is right before our jaded eyes.
How many of our friends have we ever seen
not with eyes that look over   past   beyond
but with the eyes of a photographer
an artist
a lover
You.

When familiarity evokes a yawn
and we settle down to blindness
give us the chance
and the will
to see anew with tourist eyes
the sheer beauty of a patch of yellow
in a field of green lespedeza
bowing
bending unashamed
all the wonderful sights
all the lovely people
the saint beside
the sinner within
and as much of the glory as we can take

amen.

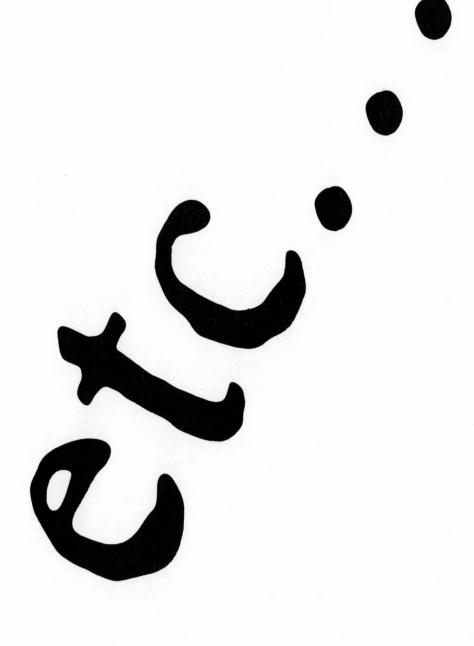

The Sun Thanks You Burning

Thank You kindly
for everything we see and hear
all the bright
gray
shiny
freckled
resonant
dissonant miracles
that we photograph and record.

Thank You kindly
THAT we see and hear
and
that there is so much more
there
here
than we have had the sensitivity to perceive.
Make us appreciative see-ers and listeners.

Thank You kindly
for what we do
and
that there is more to do than time accords.
Lord, as frustrating as it is
to never finish our lists of things to do
how tragic it would be if we could say
"All our lists are finished
all our dreams are dreamt."

Thank You kindly
for our BEING here and now
that at this point in eternity
existence   being   and life are ours.

Kind Lord
the sun thanks You burning
the moon reflectively
clouds sail thanks
water wetly praises
and we . . .
shall become who we are

amen.

True Confession

Holy God—
wholly Other
wholly Good
hear our confession.
We confess that we don't know how to confess
for we have admitted sins we haven't committed
prayed prayers so broad and vague
they've covered everything
and blushed at nothing.
We have felt guilty about the wrong things
like breathing
or just being alive
or feeling inferior all over the place
and innocent about
real wrong we have done
or
real good we have not done.
When we have asked Your forgiveness for real sins
we must admit that we have no intention of giving them up
because we're so fond of them
or so used to them
we wouldn't know how to live without them.

Do not forgive us for wondering
why
our unrepentant confessions
have left us unhealed.
Do forgive
what each of us
can honestly bring to You
that is real
and really grieved
and willing to die

amen.

We Overstand Too Much

God anew
if it were the first spring
we could hardly believe it.
Who can believe a tulip
understand rebirth
comprehend renascence
or imagine transubstantiation?
But we have outlived so many springs
we hardly notice.
Or we may analyze the botanical process
but miss the mystery.

Sensitize us to
every stirring of life
every return of warmth
every victory over the grave
Resurrection and every resurrection.
Right where we live
is as new as Eden and so stunning
but where we are
is not the only place
and there are springs far away
that we have never seen
nor ever will
that are more stunning still.
Are our mountains any less beautiful because
mountains are beautiful elsewhere?

Lord of nature
and human nature
make us most sensitive to
those for whom April is a mockery of hope
those crushed by depression made worse by a birdsong
those too overwhelmed by injustice to see fair spring
the wild
the lonely
the unalive—
in praying for them
we pray for ourselves and
intercession and petition are one

amen.

Ubiquity

We who are shepherded
enfolded
who pray from sanctuary
intercede for:
our brother far away
and our sister near at hand;
all who are sacrificed unwillingly and unwittingly
on altars of nationalism;
the priest and politician and populace
that willingly and wittingly
live on death;
the child who starves in an American slum;
the adult who eats herself into obese oblivion
in an American penthouse;
the parents of the unwanted child
whose birth brings shame;
the parents of the coveted child
whose never being born brings guilt.

Christ in the wound
Christ in the physician
Christ in the hurt and the healing
Christ in the Fat Lady
Christ in the thin woman
Christ in the wrinkled face of Mother Teresa
Christ in the wrinkled face of the dying child in her arms
Christ in the counselor and in the paranoid
Christ in the sanctuary
and in the fugitive
homeless
refugee
hounded heart—
Christ of the last
the least
the lost
inescapable   unremitting   witting   Christ—
love Yourself
in us

amen.

When the Deprivation's Done

Liberating God, who wills us free
break our bondage
for we equate freedom with
narrow escapes
postponement of judgment
stays of execution.
We visit the hospital
pass death in the halls
and vow to change our lives;
we leave the lobby
enter the sunlight
flee with relief
and forget.
God
what do we do with our freedom
when the deprivation's done?

Again and again
we lay down layers of scar tissue over wounds
we get by
we make it through our days
neither whole nor well.

Friend of freedom—
whose law goes below the deed to the motive
who would clean our hearts
and not our hands alone
who would heal the bitterness
fear   paralysis   sin
and rage
still within us
breeding
like cancer of the soul—
free us to know that
we will do nothing with our freedom
unless the wounds are healed
from the in - side
out.
Come in
and
help us out

amen.

While There's Still Time

"A great deal of water is flowing underground
which never comes up as a spring."
That's true, Lord—of us.
Sometimes we like to imagine that we are autonomous
captains of our fate
independent sorts . . .
until we reflect
and remember
father   mother   family   teacher   friends   enemies
a person
another
yet others
a "cloud of witnesses"
our own cheering section
so many who gave us so much, who cared so doggedly.

And
if we didn't say "thank you"
You know the reasons:
we didn't know at the time
we couldn't real - ize until later or too late
what he gave
how much she mattered
how different our lives became . . .
we were too shy to say it . . .
we were afraid to admit our weakness, our need, our dependence.

The gratitude WAS there
underground
even when it didn't surface.
That's a comfort . . .
and a sadness . . .
and a shame
for isn't open rebuke better than hidden love?
What was the consequence of gratitude felt but unsaid
for him who never knew
and needed so much to know
and for us who never spoke the word?
IS love unexpressed . . . LOVE?

"Let us now praise famous men"
and forgotten women

all the saints, domestic or famous.
Our debt is incalculable;
our gratitude is late in surfacing.
May it be, Lord
in time

amen.

Wholly Beautiful

God of beauty
seen in burning bush
whorled pigment
dancer's leap—
whose greatest beauty is Your holiness—
forgive us all
when we turn righteousness into self-righteousness
when we imagine that goodness must be dull
and morality oppressive
when we cast saints in plaster
and turn the beauty of holiness
into the ugliness of condemnation.

We thank You
for all the saints
whose lives were works of art
for prophets of old
far away
and good folks
close at hand
without whom
You would have given up
on the whole world
and on us.
We are more indebted than ever we know
to those who fought injustice
forgave mightily
worked and prayed for peace
said NO to sin
and
YES to love
and
reflected Your light in their lives and ours.

Maybe WE are meant to be good for others too.
Love us
into loveliness
fair and free.
In Christ's holy, beautiful name we pray

amen.